W9-CUI-761

Desire in L.A.

Desire in L.A.

Poems by
Martha Clare Ronk

The University
of Georgia Press
Athens and London

© 1990 by Martha Clare Ronk
Published by the University of Georgia Press
Athens, Georgia 30602
All rights reserved
Designed by Betty Palmer McDaniel
Set in Walbaum
The paper in this book meets the guidelines for
permanence and durability of the Committee on
Production Guidelines for Book Longevity of the
Council on Library Resources.

Printed in the United States of America
94 93 92 91 90   5 4 3 2 1

Library of Congress Cataloging in Publication Data
Ronk, Martha Clare.
    Desire in L.A. : poems / by Martha Clare Ronk.
        p.   cm.
    ISBN 0-8203-1175-8 (alk. paper). —
    ISBN 0-8203-1176-6 (pbk. : alk. paper)
    I. Title. II. Title: Desire in L.A.
  PS3568.O574D4 1990
    811'.54—dc20   89-34552
                        CIP

British Library Cataloging in Publication Data available

To the memory of my mother and father

Acknowledgments

The author and publisher gratefully acknowledge the
following publications in which these poems, sometimes in
earlier versions, first appeared.

American Poetry Review: "An exhibition of Gorky," "Looking at a
  reproduction of *Ladies of the Village,*" "One needs," "Dark
  tonight"
Antioch Review: "It's a desert still"
Bennington Review: "Sort of a country western"
Chicago Review: "Genji no. 4," as "The old woman sends her love
  poem to Genji"
Dreamworks: "Still life with brass bowl"
Georgia Review: "Reading Sappho"
Hudson Review: "The Seitz Theater"
Poetry Loves Poetry: "Nishijin," "Still life with brass bowl," "An
  exhibition of Gorky"
Southern Review: "The painting for my mother"
Sulfur: "Ironic dialogue"
Temblor: Rhetoric poems 1–8, "Still life for my mother"

Contents

The Seitz Theater

Door to door

He came to the door selling knowledge
in bound books he'd had to lug up
the unsteady stone steps
sent by someone in Georgia to Vermont
to get five credits for just even
explaining to housewives how categories
are arranged: American history,
new math and old just in case,
how to write a paragraph—some things,
he explained, never change
so it's best to get them hardbound
and have them right at hand and also
a cookbook with five thousand recipes
pages special coated so if you
spatter by accident you can just
take a cloth and wipe them clean.
In one part how to take SATs,
and in another how to use curry,
and I kept still and didn't tell him
I didn't live in the house anyhow
and the men who did lived with each other
and there weren't any schoolkids
and I hated to cook and felt so sorry
for his having been sent, ignorant,
to a state he would never know,
I sat on the stoop with him an hour
and let him spill things on the pages
and read aloud all we had in common,
the entire list of presidents,
and wiped my hands on my jeans

as if my whole front were apron,
my hands deep in pie flour,
bunches of kids hovering around
eager to have what he had to sell.

The Seitz Theater

Back of the silver screen in Sandusky
my Uncle Clinton and his wife Florence
stayed the night in a small wooden room lent
by the family before his annual sermon
at Grace Church downtown. So I'd think of him
living behind, "nay beyond," the technicolor
romances I saw there. After moving into
dark velvet spaces for an entire afternoon
my sisters and I would see what we never
got to see at home: huge lipsticked faces
kissing and the hairy necks of pirates,
their bloused shirts my first taste
of the seductive fabric of the world.
I pulled my socks up to cover my legs
and pulled my skirt down. After,
we'd wait for the dim lights and make our way
to the narrow stairs left of the screen
where Clinton would sit with Bible in hand,
his black clothes smelling of smoke.
Three pipes lined up seemed
to give order to the ashy room, the abruptness
of mortality I felt. On screen
no one was ever this old. We fingered things
and nodded until mother came to fetch us
for another technicolor, sunset ride
to Put-in-Bay. It was larger than life
this summertime in Ohio,
and even this little man, nineteen years
older than my mother, had his own bright moment
on stage. Still I hear him next day saying

God's grace would come pouring out like water
from a great pitcher in the sky. It must be
Lake Erie water I thought each summer
after the same sermon, as I plunged,
in my first bikinis, into redemption and sin.

Vermont

The man next door came after three bitter days
chewing on it in galling silence to ask:
thinking to expand your land are you?
The weeds next to his abandoned cans had been
cut down, his child was dying of what his first
had died of, no one was left to take on
the farm, the cows, the right to swallowed anger
that kept his wife from thanking his neighbors
for a flower bed that filled up year after year
with more purple than even the Catholic church
had to offer in its rows of lilacs, more than
one could bring oneself to thank anyone for.

Sanibel Island

Lizards crawl the screen again, it's Sanibel August,
before my mother dies, my father dies,
my son gets lost on the beach.
Everyone drinks before lunch—
retirees, their thin skulls burned in spots,
their wives wearing seabird golf skirts.
Dozens come into St. Luke's thrift shop, almost new.

My mother's walled herself in with pelicans;
on every surface they grin back
at those of us balancing plastic cups.
We swim in a bay hotter than a bath,
the babies lap it up, the big ones
collect pails of shells: turkey wings,
angel wings, conch, and cat's paw.

Returning boats point mast fingers up,
and the party giggles at the same lewd joke.
We drink gin. The sky dims.
When he wanders off and no one can find him;
I promise the promise of dread
at his body adrift on the waves:
I'll give up all that I have.

Stumbling back to grandma's hours later
he's burned raw by the sun.
We sit and watch lizards. Everything's askew.
A symbol of Christ, a pelican's what
we choose for the memorial window.
My mind falters and floods
as the church, shaped like Noah's ark turned
upside down, welcomes all God's creatures in.

Landmarks

Gnawed trees mark the turn
onto county crossroads
to Wilmington, Beaver's Field,
in the dark so hidden you'd miss it.
Jagged outlines like sculpture gone berserk,
these trees stand knee-deep in water, drowned.

You have to have lived here all your life
to know where the landmarks are,
top o' the hill motel,
the only bright spot for miles
on a hogback so steep
trucks lose their brakes

or here at the crossroads—
trees lost in the backdrop of night—
by feel alone
like lovers who turn
by some signal that shifts them
effortlessly in their sleep

like driving onto a hidden road
wishing at least once
to see animals building up mud flats,
paddling their felled logs,
one body's next to another,
the sign of trees, a remembered turn.

July 4

I was fifteen, say. This puffy-faced woman, wife
and mother of six, held on to her shaky drink
as if it were the anchor of the boat
her husband raced alone and loud into the Sound
each Sunday noon. I necked with the oldest
by a glass case of rifles and watched
the middle boys shoot each other with shaving cream.
From the dock he lit illegal fireworks
and turned the sky red, white, and blue,
feeling up anyone who'd come under the awning
by the back door while the hired help unloaded
six-packs of beer. Wired as I was at that age
I woke in the night and went for milk. She sat
yawning at the melting ice, while I
pert with my knowledge of pain, talked at her
until dawn. A year later she smoked in bed
and went up with the sheets.
That July we'd played a game:
a match put to gunpowder striped across paper
starts them off and the greyhounds
dash to the ends of their short lives.

Mothlike

A moth bangs hard against the shade
all sense of direction lost,
drunken bit of cloth disturbs not
because it's in the way, but is without way,
unable in the dimness to find where it means to go,
like adolescent elbows against a doorjamb,
unstable enterprise of size and weight

as once I leapt from second-floor room to room
tripped and fell headlong
into a crowd of cigarettes, highballs,
caught in a dazzle of blinding light,
and lost, seemingly forever, a sense I'd had,
just then, of flight, before my body
took over and plunged against railings

step over step to the bottom where
my mother's skirt about my shoulders
I couldn't imagine how to get to shoes
I could balance in, much less beauty,
but those wraparound wings my mother lent
buoyed me momentarily to belief,
a mothlike dependence on eventual sun and grace.

Spanish moss in America

Spindly white threads hang in the greenhouse,
Spanish moss, no host,
but like all of their kind needing
just air, as the grass needs cutting,
as surely as it rains
the rocks in the stream the road goes by
grow up out of water where a boy
in red hand-me-downs dams up a river,
holds an invisible stick
striped like a flag, small-town
American barber pole, his hair
cut flat against his head,
clambers a bit and finally
sits still holding the day
in his white hands.
Of course you don't have to
go fishing with your father but
he'll be hurt but the boy didn't
want real fish that squirmed and flapped
like his own body swimming,
like a dream he's had
of having to pull slippery weeds
from the water for days
out of murky bottoms until
the stream runs clear,
hating mud more than his father
who stood back there
in the garage waxing the car
listening to ball games until
it all went dreamy and he didn't

remember having a family of boys
but being a boy drifting
through streams of childhood
and hanging off the edges of cliffs
like pictures he's seen of Spanish moss.

John Henry

He knew what it meant to come up to the mark,
set quotas for himself and meet them, year after year,
return with a pin or a pen from Toledo.
When I asked what they did there, my mother shrugged
and said well we probably didn't want to know

and felt the relief women feel
that you could feed the children something cold
now no one was coming home tired, hungry,
daylight lasting longer in the yard,
hands deeper in the soil of her garden,
she went lax in the bath,
talcum all over her back

and we rolling down the lawn like waves
until our knees were grass-stained green
eating stuffed eggs to the rhythm of
swaying feet under the formica table,
a woman and three girls,
the household reverting to female,
the focus in his absence
blurred like late afternoon.

After his work was gone,
his punctiliousness confusedly not enough,
he set his jaw to the sea
we had followed in his wake to,
promoted early, retired soon, left on the shore
with two boats, three cars, and nothing to do.

At night he'd pick beans off his plate

as if he'd never seen food,
his girls gone out he didn't want to know where,
and sit on the seawall staring out
or rake seaweed off the beach,
setting himself the impossible task
of keeping it clear of what the sea washed in,
her careless and prolific abandon
more than a match for one man.

Dark tonight

Waiting for it three hours so I can throw the switch,
save the house and pump, thunder finally sounds
from far off, though I had known from the thin voice
over the wire, it would come.

Nothing distracts my breath-held fear,
and the dog lolls and snores or like the radio jumps
with static in its sleep dreaming of a quieter time.
All the power in the world. It will be dark tonight.

Sitting with my mother dying in her own bed, I remember
she told how hurricanes forced them from the island,
past the frightened herons, spoonbills, cranes,
and those poor birds born frail into a world without oiled
    wings—

we saw them on drives through the sanctuary,
the ones she took us on when we came south to visit,
their feathered heads drooping, their brown bodies
and wings outspread, hanging themselves up in dark
    branches to dry.

Nishijin*

When we got lost the man from the elegant shop
who spoke little English said left at the Chinese
for Raku. You said, how the hell will we know
one from the other; without the plastic food
they all look Japanese.
                              But we chanced a left
and the museum, displaying a large pink poster pot,
just what we wanted, was closed. I wanted so much
from you after all these years: girlhood and lawns,
no husbands, no children, nobody dead.

Walking arm in arm in skirts through narrow streets
I wanted to twirl until cloth stood out
from skinned knees, until freeze tag, until bed.

You think I remember too much, your children
crawl in and out of your lap, you stiffen
when I'm up early too. But that one day
when we got lost and didn't find Raku,
had to break down and take a cab, we laughed
until we cried and heard the steady whirr
of looms making cloth behind closed doors.

*Nishijin is the name of the silk-weaving district in Kyoto

Italy wins at world soccer

In Rome I met a schoolteacher
who acted exactly as she was supposed to
came from Florida, had given up
having her hair done, wore flat shoes
and carried her valuables in a plastic sack
so as no one would know anything important
was in there and ate between dusk
and dark in the kitchen at the end
of the hall when even I was brave
enough to eat out by myself and on
the bus to St. Peter's she hugged
her stuff close to her chest
because that bus had pickpockets
on it and a nun had been knocked
over in the streets by a boy
on a motorbike who grabbed at her purse
and broke her hip and then she walked
to the Protestant cemetery to give
flowers to Keats and then walked through
all the Vatican gardens and the museums
and saw everything long after all
of us got tired and went for naps
or beers or watching soccer on tv
hearing the radios blare behind
dark doorways, and she kept going while
the red and green and white flag
dragged through the streets and boys
threw boys into fountains and Italy
won.

Rhetoric

Rhetoric no. 1

Does one tire of rhetoric, ever?
Shall we get lost on the freeway together,
love, stare at the Market Basket moon,
caught as always in electric wires,
a tangle of sentences about motion,
tv, or crystalline Marxism, which kind,
and where can we find a couch that feels
at home, unsettled as the cushions are.
Sweet Peace, where have you got to
in this reign? When I got the notion
of it, it was too late, that's what's at fault,
timing, gait, the inability to read signs
on the connection between Pasadena, Silverlake,
the way you are when you can't control
almost everything and how you worry
about lying, the smallest, really, of sins.

Rhetoric no. 2

I can't utter, I began, a simple truth,
utterance without the mental cloud of
"it's impossible to know," utter nonsense,
and the likelihood of betraying what
two seconds previously passed
like those "real" clouds, watching
from a lawn marked by a live oak, two streets,
skirts spread out like fans as exotic as truth,
sky, death. I've mimicked the stuttering
of a student who says, eloquently,
he is wed to language, nevertheless,
suffering her veil, her ruthless eyes,
saying, "I do, I do," until the utter end
of time, sucking on collapsing teats,
and still remembering ecstasy.
"Very like a camel," I said incredulously,
stale perception come upon me newly,
like your lead weight that keeps me
simply, from evaporating, lying.

Rhetoric no. 3

Why does "it" rain, it's raining, or it's wet
everywhere, why does "it" hurt, displacement
away from the center of what can't be
conceived—self, sky, what's up there somewhere
bringing to or toward, a finger cut
slicing a hunk of bread, "she" grows faint, "we"
lie on the floor by the green rug,
"I" forget about it until washing a plate
it aches and suddenly it's pouring floods of
childhood somersaults into the French doors,
blood on the carpet I said was the sea.
But who was it stood upright there
by the rain gutter near the oak tree?
Who would have thought the faint wail
of a freight train would be memory not fact,
the pain of losing it all clearing like rain.

Rhetoric no. 4

It doesn't matter, let it go, washed off
queerness of the moment, how unsettled
the weather makes days of rain and damp
settled into bedclothes, minds clogged
with the inability to think straight through,
memory coming on us like clouds dropped
about the farmhouse so he drops the glass
on the brick floor and we hunt in the dark
for slivers of light, say it doesn't matter,
can't stop thinking of the child who fell
to the ground, a blackening triangle,
pain in his crumpling knees, in the voice
I hear over the crackling wire, he wants me,
I want to be with child, chill breaks
ordinary needs for food or ease, leaving
only an ache in Bressonian wrists and arms.

Rhetoric no. 5

Like rhetoric memory's fashioned of whirls,
embellished meringues dissolving on the tongue,
I hear her voice in the scarabs she wears
heavily in the dream before they're stolen
by men at the piano bar, they tip their hats,
we've met before, remember the evening we "dined"
before what's his name in Richard III.
A genoise's made without baking powder,
comes into being for a birthday I see in newsprint
come off on my hands as I wrap presents,
tie them with string. What's decadent, he asks,
turning almost fifteen, what's love?
Since you said his name on the phone
I've dreamed of him seven times,
lost him seven times more,
given speeches with closed mouth to cakes and clothes
as if laundry could get up and walk, tailor-made.

Rhetoric no. 6

Night climbs into my forced horizon,
limb by creaking limb. Who goes there or
lift up your lanthorn, buddy, let me pass.
Oh, he says, in the imitation voice
of a jazz musician: fuck it, falsetto,
fuck it, out back is where I live, musty
and let me carry the voice of old Virginia or
any other influenced by Gullah and games.
My skill at hopscotch reduced to marginal notes
or what's left in the left hip no one can hear
except like the lilt of a song she says,
Jacksonville is where I come from
and not till the words drop away
does the sound make itself known
like ribbing on a transatlantic hull.
Who would leave where growing up
occurs as if it were obvious?

Rhetoric no. 7

To believe whose talk or later in the day
walking is beyond anyone's description,
ache in the loins, loitering where the bus
stops for each gullible man, sleeves rolled,
untethered ramble lurks in the mouth,
pronouncements rapid as mosquitoes buzz—
who's one to have faith in—
concentration and confidence are and have been
undermined, Melville, James, and Whitman knew
and what tradition is this we partake of,
eating garlic, chilis, sweet onions
and pretending to be out on the town
entertaining multitudes in Italy, Spain.
Here, soon as I hit the sofa I sleep,
even in the middle of a lecture
can't remember what I was to say
about *The Making of Americans*, America itself.
Yet someone had a big moustache,
looked like Mark Twain and it wasn't just
makeup, a big roller of a big cigar.

Rhetoric no. 8

Before the time, dying before one's
cantilevered out and dangling, this sly
purchase on a view, who's to say what might be
seen. Sitting on a pier I saw no leap
but the circles after, my son said, there's
a fish, oh see its feathers, but I said
the crane that walks the steamy lawn
at breakfast might have if you were close enough
but fish have, and he replied: time was
once upon fish flew across painted sky
landed with mouths open to the air
swallowing and denying that three doors down
his grandmother breathed her last
and lifted her fingers across the sheets
like the legs of self-conscious birds,
awkward pencil-drawn stick feet extending
into a future, a blank page, blue lines
like veins and what's to come ever the past.
I Squanto teach you to plant blue corn.
I Pilgrim marvel at the many fishes.

Epigrams

1.
I fast and take to bed trying to forget
the only cure for you is gluttony and
your slow-moving limbs.

2.
The Olympia stares out at all men as if
you were the only one
she'd put the finger on.

3.
Since you now address me only in public,
and only in front of others, I contemplate
running for sudden office.

4.
It doesn't mean a thing, I protest, that I give you
jewels and pearls. Of course I want you
prostrate before me.

5.
He doesn't want to see her suffer or look sad,
so, smug, he ditches her, admonishing, be glad.

6.
I suppose that when I think of it
I'll laugh like van Gogh's crows
mourning over fields of bright wheat.

7.
Each time I see you you're more beautiful
than before. Your stance less artful,
having been more carefully rehearsed.

8.
Men have one chance to please us,
usually before or after is best:
take your pick.

9.
We rush in where we know we shouldn't,
taking pleasure in the squeezing in—
only later the pinch of memory.

10.
You're thinking in that vulgar mode again,
my sweet, and your hands wander as they often do.
Keep your thoughts to yourself.

11.
When I speak to you my heart beats hard,
tries courageously to fly from its cage
to the net you freely proffer.

12.
Your self-assurance these days appalls me:
You know you've got me where you want me,
and I know the effort I put out getting there.

13.
He thinks his soul is buried in some hell or other;
in truth he worries lest the match he lights
might singe his beautiful lashes.

14.
Narcissus looked into the mirror of his face;
what he found there, the last thing he wished to embrace.

15.
Now that my woman's softness has helped you go off
to confront what's hard, what, my love,
shall I do with my own hard feelings?

Exhibitions

An exhibition of Gorky

I've always seen those things
in abstract paintings but was embarrassed to say so and
now you tell me it's the newest theory about Gorky himself
that he wasn't solving problems about latter-day cubism
wasn't figuring out relationships of shapes
but was putting down that leaned-over ass just as I thought
all those toilets or at least the paper looks like porcelain
to me and that red smudge is certainly death anyone can see
    that
and the green horned fuzz in the corner of that cheery one
is a sheep, it is a sheep, the whole work: pastorale.

                                        Too bad
he couldn't've just stayed there but kept me moving while
that flowerlike scrawl of a lily turned metallic
turned flying petals of tin
knifed him in the back.

Still life with brass bowl

Like the dreams I had taking naps, flying
about the wallpapered room gazing at tea roses
and yellow ribbons wrapping up the wall
and keeping me from flying out the window
avoiding the corner of the southwest room
I pivoted and hung; the brass bowl polished
to a sheen sits so near the table edge
it would fall to the floor if it didn't float.
Like a miracle. The fir in the corner
grows in each photograph until it is larger
than the house, until I am completely grown,
changed by increments through time like the face
of my father in the hospital bed resting
with half a brain for the last time.

A photograph as good as a picture

(from a photograph by Ruth Orkin)

He leans forward with such
fervor, yet isn't young, and something
decidedly is happening, even
to the beefy fellow in his white
short-sleeved shirt. A photograph—
oh, perhaps not the same as a
Manet, but it is Auden, and
for whatever reason he stares at
the square flesh neckline
of her dress. He is forward
in his chair, rumpled about
the collar, and everyone is wearing
black and white. It is the formal
occasion of how much he cares
to be there, Venice, 1951,
and how much I care to see him
no matter what for, longing
like that.

Looking at a reproduction of
Ladies of the Village in T. J. Clark, a letter

Behind the stiff ladies in their stuff of satin,
the landscape may be, as he says,
laid on in too thick a palette,
"foliage and cliff-edge blurred to a froth of paint,"
but the fault may be not in the thing itself,
but an idea that anyone can get it straight
even Courbet, observing sister, dog and cow,

since now, as the storm comes on me slowly
by the incremental brightening of bird call
and the hush and eddying of wind,
my sense of how to describe it in this letter
to you, city-bound and precise, is—
no matter I could walk ten paces and put a hand
on the split maple—blurred.

So quickly a mystery, just beyond
a drift of rhododendron at the end of their pale bloom,
green turns metaphoric, black trunks recede
into a smear of rotted undergrowth
my straining eyes can't see. Tops of trees
spatter a sky the color aching would be,
remembered diffidence, a careless goodby.

Over the head of the barefoot girl
who reaches a limp hand for the packet of money
hangs a dark amorphous shape,
failed rendering of a cliff

even the yipping of a frothy-tailed dog can't scare.
These women in their out-of-place dress,
the particular tree out my window—
nothing jars the sense of messy failure located deeper
in the unpainted woods than I could possibly walk.

The painting for my mother

I make you buy the painting of the swans
as if it will make you live as long as it takes
all of them to enter the gold-green reeds.
They come out of the nowhere of marshland and float
under the vast sky. The tumor is smaller
on the X rays this month; the doctors are
pleased. I fly to Florida for your birthday,
your face as white as mine, your mind wandering.
Both daughters give you talismans
disguised as gifts: one a Chinese bell on blue string,
one a porcelain necklace with painted birds—
long-legged birds for longevity—their wings
open across a white sky, flying in place.

Still life for my mother

(after reading *Chardin and the Still-Life Tradition*)

The glinting of musical instruments and eggs
and oranges and meat pies, how simple it all was
then, no one coveted anything I thought
in the world of still life painting and everything
held still: *quoe virtus et quanta sit/*
vivere parvo with cheese and petals falling
to the table.
                          She's dying this year for us all.
It has gathered into her chest. The petals
on the table are beautiful, the artichoke;
Cezanne, it says, was hungry for bread.
                                        What could I give up,
what would it take. Take all the flowers
from every still life vase. I'd grow purple iris
across the entire countryside of southern France.

The winter before last

In the winter before last photo he preens
to be taller and won't wear gloves—
the rest of us are freezing and the cousin
he used to scorn for brushing her hair
mindlessly 50 times before going to bed
before beating him at Risk
is looking up at her mother whose eyes
are closed and at me who is also
for the first time in 15 years looking up.

The boy has dragged his arm about my shoulder
from above; the stripes on his polo shirt stretch.

I'm back at wishing for him as hard as
when he was born. It's a threshold as chancy—
not just the body thrust on him wantonly
as before, but what to do
when it's up against others
with the size and desires of a man
among women who want only to win or get out.

Like a photograph

My son stands in iron-rust water,
the grasses are August high,
artemesia silvers the hill, I never

want to be anywhere else. He hits fourteen,
taller than anyone now, standing back
to back, sliding a flat hand. The garden

has gone its measured course from yellow to blue
and back to yellow again.
For me it is the end of Vermont.

My sister says, it must be the beginning of summer.
In the water his legs foreshorten and waver;
we are in the circus-mirror of our dreams—

women, sisters, children, men.
This, if I could have named it, is what I looked into
as a child and thought, one day I'll be taller, there

where my mother stands up to her knees in the lake.
Now her narrow back belongs to the rest of us,
her stories of an animal living

under the bed are passed to the boy, to his stepsister
just towns away. Already the water in the rocky stream
colors us sepia brown.

Corot

Lights come on in the Mediterranean sandstone town
as our eyes get used to the paint,
each daub of white brightening
as the invisible woman behind the wall
puts a match to kerosene,
her nose wrinkling at the acrid smell.

Gravel leads to buildings
clumped behind tops of lightly brushed trees,
an obstruction of green.
A river passes beneath a Roman bridge,
in and out of finger-weeds
like longing, inching toward

salmon-colored stone.
It shivers like a cold swimmer.
One odd bush shoves up against the picture plane
as full as any pod opening its milkweed
into scraggly fields.
Burst of white. Impeded desire.

Black seeds parachute into what could be France
it's so far away. Everyone speaks a foreign tongue.
The light on the grass lures us on.
How long would it take to get to
the woman singing to herself,
bare skin rubbing against nettles and dry sage?

Drawings by Seurat

Where the charcoal is missing
the blank page is skin as erotic as
the book is lying on my lap
what did you mean leaving
the boy posing for Seurat
sitting in for not so far away
mannerisms of late night
everyone has to be somewhere.
I worry the thread of the unraveling book.
"If the self is private the overcoming
will take the form of violating that privacy."
If you are forbidden to read it
keep it under wraps
walk in painstaking steps to the park.
Boys are already fishing
and color's come out
on the women's skirts.

Still life: iconography

Used to be each item stood for, death's head
stood for, a shell. The vanity of human wishes
everywhere displayed.
She poked her finger through eye sockets,
meditated her desire for wanting
to drop the edge of her blouse over one shoulder.
Put on the table the identical jug
like the kitchen jug, like beer, like tobacco,
like something eternally missing.
The pipe: is it more than the possibility
of stoned dreams, the pleasure of a smoke after dinner,
vague ingenuity of man: a bowl, a stem?

Distortions

photographs by Kertesz

All nudes are distorted
and here we are taking off our clothes
again.
                I knew someone once
who wore silk kimonos to bed every night
but more often it's this problem of

                fitting together
seeing how the crooks are to go
and in the dark.

And illusions we carry, his that I am wise enough
to impart it through the skin. Mine
that his warmth will make me unafraid
for days and mirrored days.

Of course we're not to blame,
it's the angle of knees to back,
                of elbow to hair

how crooked we all appear and undefined
as if the brush forgets how to make
a straight line, as if

                long ago

I was having trouble in school
because I couldn't see the blackboard.

Reading Sappho

Of course her thighs, of course the way she gasps
when some Spartan strolls languidly by. Of course
she can't get enough of skin. Days later you delay

telling me how beautiful the words are, how sweaty
they make your palms. You remind me how you
respond after the fact. Watching your thin beauty

I recall Sappho's full lips, the plentitude
of her smile. She imagines women with multiple legs
jumping into the comic sea. Water fills up with them.

We walk a tightrope. If the time is right
we wonder whether we should say what's on our minds.
Your hair is fine-lined, my fingers knotty bone.

The flesh of Greek women fills the room. We leave
thin wrists behind, cross out whatever is written
about us. A fat woman stoops to fasten a strap.

Elgin Marbles

Their shoulders lie back in their sockets, they
insist on warmth, throw off drapery; their skin
looks hot. Innocent, uncouth,
they ask all of us to come touch them,
pull off their marble clothes.

                              Once
I saw a shoulder like that on a girl
larger than her age who knew how to come on,
disdained anyone who'd lay a hand on her.

Blouses the color of naked skin, she cut
her hair completely off and sat
absolutely still: no one could touch her.

                          This time
in the vast hallway when the guard's back
was turned, I put my hand on the shoulder
of someone whose name is not known for sure.

Lady Emma Hamilton as La Baccante

Famous for her series of *poses plastiques,*
she exposes a breast to the world,
hair unkempt, unlikely flowers and twigs
dropped over her brow, a full fruity mouth.
She ought always to have been so richly endowed
with the innocent power of a high-colored cheek.
"She died in distress and want."

And how many men had her.
"Employed in some doubtful capacity
by a notorious quack of the time," she went on
to painters drawn by the fascination of skin
rising to any occasion.

One traded her to an uncle for debts,
her debt always her sex,
the coinage of ever-ripening skin,
what she did brilliantly beneath her skirts,
becoming a Lady, marrying what she'd already had.

Hooked on risky business,
trading one man for his better,
she turned her glow on Nelson
returned with success of his own from the Nile,
her tongue in his mouth, her child in his bed,
and went on to the world of fortune,
gambling with a passion hotter than lust.

How she mocked his efforts to curb her.
Did they think, when the sitting was done,
the bedding complete,

breakfast brought in on a silverish tray,
she would rise, say thank you, and stop?

Extravagance was a skill of sorts
like the overgrown garden she wears
on her head in this one,
or "habits profuse she contracted in Naples,"
catching everything in the open mouth
of beauty and greed, headlong like one of her kind
into final and abundant ruin and want.

Still life: to name, to want

They thought to name themselves: basket of,
fruit and, the pipe, the peach, the pane.
Someone is looking out of, her bouquet fails.
One looks like a cupboard, open, dangling
its keys; inside there is music written out
on paper, two books, what looks to be jam.
The lid shuts forever. No one will get in
but the invitation will suggest itself,
insinuate, obsess, and our longing will grow
over time for wanting to get in, get in,
not the cupboard, not even the frame.
No one even reaches the room the painting
is hanging in, the hallway, the door, the room.

One needs

One needs perhaps someone who doesn't have to
think about it because she was born quietly
or wore a tweed jacket with silk showing
at the sleeves or because yellow suited
his post-structuralist position and rank.
Or one finds oneself drawn despite irony
to those with an aw-shucks shuffle.
This is part of the city's liability,
the New Yorker says: one needs grounding;
believe what you see. Of course they were hung
too close together. Of course there's need for
big-time murder. Of course we're addicted to
swagger and fall. Yet, looking for a way to shuck
the husk of habit, take on some distance
and stance, return to what one knows:
the beauty of a veined foot tossing a slipper aside.
One needs these like sentimentality,
the soft-spoken visitor from Japan,
language with the personal pronouns still.
I see it almost touching the ground.

The object of desire

The elaborate celibate twilight
fog entrapped between trees
orifices filled with leggy things insisting.
Macbeth kills instead.
The driveway apron edged by heather
name of pen pal at eleven
no more or less than now
casual acquaintance for focus.
The calf steams and ruts
birthing flies from her forehead
slowly toward the corral of death.
The mountains succumb to acid illness
it's an airborne illusion.
The nods enclose distance
on a road to arbitrariness
catching a glimpse of
what to see today.
Sitting as still as
married to a deep knowledge of chess
remembering a man as beautiful
playing under a nameless tree.
Arborvitae to stop the play of mind
desire implies being seen by someone else
making do with mirrors
Diana as the object of Actaeon's imagination
an operation of occular possession
which is culminated instead
by staying indoors
and letting it blow over.
Veils necessary for voyeurism
what anchoring an unnamed green

left by the fall of pale blooms
ringing the stones of the state.
The branches he couldn't possess
kingly undoing in a vision
enveloped by anomalies
women with beards
chaste uncoupled things
seen or unseen by groundlings
lineage patronizing authorship
telling her to do it
which cost her her sons
the eternal daughter swaddled up.

Tale of Genji poems

1.

Giggling we don't come out
from behind the screen; we peer at those passing
as if they were ghosts of the fifth rank.
Only women here.
                    Her hair is as long as
the emperor's long life; when she covers her mouth
to laugh, powder comes off in her hand.
We live together in twilight, slide from
one pile of silk to another. The smallest girl
buries herself in robes and never
wakes up. She has bad dreams she says
and refuses to blacken her teeth.

We tell the same stories again and again.

2.

You come across the rain-drenched courtyard
as if you had never seen rain.
            When you stand
beneath the willow your body sways
with the wind. Your arms hang down
like branches filled with water.
A servant girl arranges rocks to please you,
turns the stream slightly aside.

Tears brighten your eyes, the beautiful rain
stops.
            Even when I turn away into the main house
there is no way I can take my eyes off you.

3.

Ever since
I thought of kissing
you, on the back of
behind your ears
                        where
so I imagined lilies and alternately
a straight long line of purple

                    iris
each day has been
the texture of days between rain
cloud-light striped between earth
and sky
                        my own longing caught
between one long strand of
                oiled hair
and another.

4.

She said, there are so many folds
in the world's screen

              behind

all the long-legged birds
I see your light shining

from behind peonies (pink,
globed)

              from behind
lilies and through the painted mountain air
on new screens where colors lie
thick and wet
or old ones, the brush strokes scraped off
by time and use.

              Even if
she said, the screen was folded
on itself, time and again
screen added to wooden screen until

              the clap of
fanlike folds rang softly in my ear, until
you were on the other side of the world

I would see your light shining.

5.

How often you stand in the doorway gazing
at some body of water
not there.
                                 Branches surround
the small pond. You wish to be somewhere
else, wish the corner of the maple leaf
would not turn brown, not yet
that Yugao had not gone to live quietly
with her husband, that you still loved me.
                                I see
you hate whatever is put
in front of you. Sweet wine is sour
on your tongue. Still
I want to lick you clean like a newborn child.

6.

It was the wrong father and finally
everyone knew it. She had
no choice but to cut her hair
and enter the gates.

            She said she didn't mind
leaving the world, her family, the fine-line eyes
of her child (she kissed them each a thousand times)
but what it meant to be a father baffled her
made her stumble as if she hadn't seen
the corner of the garden flagstone, as if she were
completely lost in thought.

            It took only a moment
this fathering. Why she knew the rough edging
on the lesser screen better than she knew
his hands.

            Before becoming a nun
she memorized the feet of her child.

7.

Your hands dart. I'm blinded
by fish crossing the hem of your kimono,
by the bright end of day.
                              Dancing
is one thing: at the festival of red leaves
you made the emperor cry
                              but this is
merely four fingers together, thumbs out.

As it comes out of the sleeve, your hand
informal, much too bright
for my unacquainted eyes.

I don't hear what you say (strangely
my mother talking, sisters bending
in the tall grass)
                              like being
the lake through which the carp swim.

8.

I am provided for, layers
of silk, baskets of
fans. I can stir the air and dress
for more occasions for more centuries
than I will ever know. I can stand
in the doorway, my hands on smooth wood,
my powdered face nodding to the powdered moon.

I'll never sing for you again, never hear
your voice.
                    When your carriage rolls away
I'll burn the grape-colored robe you gave me
on the day of the weaver star. I'll catch
the moon in the poisoned water of a silver bowl
and drink it down.

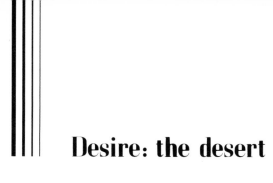

Desire: the desert

Desire in L.A.

Pull away from the map of the mind sprawls
over the whole of city streets, L.A. extends
our own errands and where we have to get to, you
are far away, left at corners where one awning tears
in the once-a-year wind, where the wind blows
the trees as we stand over the open grave,
the one we love; planes taking off from the airport.

Waves turn to go out to sea,
a whole city expanding like the universe,
each drive up canyons, each centrifugal wind reaching
beyond what used to be the limits of a city
and none of us can stop
pushing beyond our time, our money, the need
for some outskirts of a city already wholly outskirts,
reaching for, like erotic desire, the nether parts.

Mannered fingers and necks elongate beyond themselves,
skin hurts drying in the wind,
and waiting to find transparent expansion
into the upper reaches of not even belief,
but craving our own unbelief
and that image of another's skirt
lifted by the warm, slightly soiled air of an open grate.

Photographs by Walker Evans

We stop at the drive-in where coffee's
the sludge one wants after hours in a car.
Two years ago you sent me a postcard,
a desolate motel fronted by dying palms,
a portent, I thought, not of itself,
but intimacy, a language of black and white
I hadn't yet imagined, despite photographs
Evans took, despite signs of distress.

Yet who could wish for anything more
of a particular sort of embrace.
The motel windows drew me like liquid—
glass turning to reflected glass and back again—
as you do looking at me, suspicious
as any of them looking at him.

One can only wonder what they thought it was,
a record not only of anguish, but the unspoken
question of what it all might mean.
Where've you been, where're you off to,
the waitress brings another cup, sets it down
as if she'd seen herself do it.

The desert as the idea of what's missing

Sometimes it comes down to
being still as the flattest of imagined land
folding up a picture of it in your pocket
that you take out when no one's looking,
the crease across the akimbo arm of
the Joshua tree part now of
what you'd look to find there,
a smudge where you've marked the moon
with whorls of your thumb.
An entire presentation of things missing,
this expanse of dust and air
fused to one another at the horizon
like lying on top of his sleepy body
lulled like a moving car,
the earth tilted toward a sunset
I keep in my pocket and try to forget
that once I imagined cactus pears
tasted like the rosy beauty
of late daylight in and around Mohave.

The painted desert

Your love's as flat and empty as I can see from here.
It stretches like dust and other assorted minerals
into the distance: ah the blue, ah the green.
They say none of this is by accident,
it has purpose, it has sheen.
We've been arguing, it seems, for days,
can't get in a car without the future looming like road signs.
The elevator closes with a reddish glow.
My heart aches like neon at five.
After a time no one will be able to find
nature in the midst of urban sprawl.
One fenced-in tree will serve for tourists:
we'll stand in line for the chance to lie down
and stare up into some dusty mongrel sort of thing
while daydreams of the past come back in a flash.
I remember Kansas, you'll say, it was so flat.
Even in those days you couldn't find the center of town.

Inyokern

If I could describe the exact shade of confinement,
as Tanizaki's bright tarnish of silver trim
against shadowy miso, black lacquered bowl,
as we drive back into the tangle of
city life more gnarled than bristlecone,
as the day must relinquish itself,
twilight filling up the small room,
clinging with astonishing half-light
to the underside of leaves, routine.

If I could say: the air is clearer
here in Inyo, but nevertheless
we make our painful way
through mazes of trying to locate a tone
deep enough to contain behind that
a sweeter reach toward doves
calling from the palm tree before I'm awake,
long before I've come out of leaden sleep
to find the shadowy curve of your arm,
the taste of salty soup on your skin.

It's a desert still

Loving and not
occur like living in one city
and an imagined other,
driving past the moment
at which knowledge slides like hillsides
muddy into the main street,
pulling along a cactus, a clapboard house or two.

Yesterday I pretended tomorrow wouldn't come,
but not today.
That you are leaving is no accident
though when we stop to watch the train
we note only the antiquity of the caboose.
I taste you in my mouth.

Later the city is
where I never want to live,
no seasons, no home, open spaces
like open moments leaking the past:
the president shot in the laundromat
where I folded someone else's jeans.

It falls apart, then rights itself.
We sweep the desert from the streets,
cover it with concrete and pretend.
Meanwhile whole populations refuse paint
and hotels are got up not for love.

The Thomas guide breaks at the binding,
my arms ache at the joints and so forth.
The desert's never going away,
won't give up its rights to dominate the ground.

Lone Pine, CA

Named, the postcard says, for a Jeffrey pine
that later washed away, it rides the base
of the Sierras as if it too could be erased.
Hidden in tall grass I watch children dash
out of the water, creep tentatively—
hunched over with the aching cold—in.
Everyone's unsettled. It's months before I've met you.
On this day no one hits it off except
in the restless desire for too much,
the insistence that we all push up
the nearest peak at the hottest time of day,
fall asleep by strangers we've known for years,
a child crying out in the night
at unknown sounds, a sky of falling stars.

Crossings

To believe in crossovers is not the same as
having a conversation, her words left him
cold, her weakness was evident to them
both, her diligence, dilitantism, dreadful
undergarments and self-pity. She looked
at everything as if she could make statements
about it. His dry manner denied
involvement, lacrosse, that wet grass is
anything like film. You can't get that
he'd say walking across the damp ground
or moving a bar of soap across the hair
of his left arm. Soon they're taking a car
somewhere where it's hot and dry, they'll go
to the desert, to a ruin, Death Valley perhaps.

Remodelling

She put her face naked in his belly and blew smoke rings
around him, dashing her various Pall Malls to the floor
and galumphing around the room. He stared her down.
She pulled threads from socks she found on the floor,
pretended they were the small hairs on his legs
before tying the knot and vowing loyalty ever after,
after he had already gone out for more beer. Timing
wasn't her suit, she lost at cards, never put on
the right color according to some chart he'd worked out
in his mind which she imagined like a random selection
of paint-store samples. She always got stuck with
the putrid one, the unlikelihood of ever
getting around to redoing the room or else.

A celebration of love and the new year

One says "love" in bell-like tones,
aghast, having no way of knowing beforehand
it would turn out to be true.

At night they recite it and hate
the armchairs they sit in,
their brown shoes, the same last name.

Without weapons of irony, she asks,
how shall I battle his innocent smile?
He lengthens his arms and vowels

and finds her as foreign
as the chill of winter
waited for through November and March.

Light leaks under the doorjamb,
neon going on full-blaze inside,
pink tubes of it lining the walls.

A revel of tuxedos in shiny New Year's Eve
hats and horns with feathers at the end
tickles the question again.

One on the street near midnight says
something, as if the sound held in her teeth
came closest to desire.

Sort of a country western

Evenhandedly he moved toward the pink rectangle
hung across the boulevard; it was advertising something
to drink and he did.

Where will we go he said, toward what end, he thought
about the usual breaks in a sentence, about his heart and
    love.

Intermittently he saw how buildings rise up
and restaurants and how lonely he felt when he hadn't
    managed
to forget how often he had walked that street, the one over.

Lined up like nouns, names like Avocado, Orangegrove,
    Lemontree,
once in the town of Winston-Salem a street called
    Greatjones—Cigarette Row
all this order and vocabulary shifts from one part of the
    country
to another, here how hard not to repeat like gray smog and
    beer.

He talked of punching him out, wanting to break his face,
saying it over and over again, tried eating different things
for breakfast, for a time considered bacon the perfect food,
salt, sodium nitrite, fat, no nutrients at all,
the perfect Sunday, even-tempered and how it isn't good for
    you.

Ironic dialogue

You cannot give me lore of teacups, I know
your kind, she sd.
                        Sweet Jesus what d'ya think I am
a sissy?
            What cravings I've got for painted cups and tea
she moaned, twining herself, legs and all
and gazing: painted green vines, birds, all
beckoned fitfully. Oh, for a story, she sd.

                                    Jesus, I'm
hungry just for food, he clawed.

                            If you'd read
to me, I'd curl up all around you and sexy
she pulled herself out for him like blooms,
bright splotches on the glaze. I wonder
if it's true, she sd., if they have such birds,
long legs drooping and such an arching wing?
She gazed with vacant eye. Do they have bridges
over goldfish and waterlily pads?
                            You live in flimsy
dreams, he snapped.
                        Just looking at my cup, she swirled.

Unlike the movies, life is

Without subject, before adolescence, what then
is sent to us, gathers import, a clatter of dishes
from a window across the echo through the courtyard:
Columbus. Name a city, invent a tongue. Each
ransacked moment yields little more, nor more
fruitful this arranged platter of cherries, or
whiskey soda, how the hotels stack up
downtown near where each Easter they got
navy blue coats with brass buttons,
passed them down three girls pushing down
steps, throwing red berries at, dressing up in
curtains, lacy for heroines, great hats
for the men, characters spurred to revenge,
riding the plains, before the movies even.

Domestic Surrealism 1–6

1.

In domestic surrealism the chairs at discordant
angles often and surprisingly flinch, sing out
and finches and other odd birds gather about.
He tells stories of when they were young
and life was like mugs filled with foam.
She stood by the back of his chair laughing
at the same stories even when she didn't listen.
Two doves startled across a road
and there's no river, but he had seen the sea
and it was like an endless dancing floor—
boards with no chairs, only the legs of women, men,
and their beautiful soft leather shoes.
She throws off her heels on the fire escape.
One hundred kilometers east, sea birds run by.

2.

For the sake of absolute balance, on one side
of the walkway a pink bush, on the other, a white.
Her socks match her shirt. On the mantel two candlesticks
push out six inches from either wall.
Everything is like pieces of desert paper
blowing in the wind. The motel shortly disappears,
the road already comes undone, and beer cans litter
what's left of vacancy. On Saturdays there's no room
except the sky. Like a veneer of saran wrap the city
lies across the basin waiting to be rolled up,
taken to a new set of circumstances and spread out
to wait for hoards of people with weapons or without.
Everyone prances like ponies, skitters like lizards.
No wonder her silver shoes, no matter her silver hair.

3.

Suspicious, those who insist on happiness
show off their ability to eat.
I'm happily addicted to a show of hands:
how many wept before breakfast, who takes
anything but nervy jitters, styrofoam coffee,
lids torn crescent-shape to take on the road.
They serve up pasta in moon-white plates,
and everyone's invited to eat and drink,
yet misery has its flaunts and flaps,
and I'll take its loony excess over laughter
anyday, pleated cardboard over the dashboard,
the mockingbird's sad metallic sound,
practically serving up cakes and ale.

4.

It's the sofa series, chairs rearranged,
gobbled up and right there on the front porch
next to the new paint job where everyone
used to sit a spell, now who watches
the Dodge with whitewalls since grandpa died
who in many a movie played
doc or doorman or sat, can in hand,
whilst some elaborate couple passed by,
stripes on his shiny pants, one down her hose.
At the store, over a bin of pinto beans, a cane.
I'd like to sit on you and feel you squirm.
Stuffed furniture out-of-doors is how awkward I feel
every time I have the urge to do it.
At 15 my huge saddle shoes dangling
over the wooden slats, I rocked in mother's lap
while boys gangbanged a girl name of Missy Moon.
Once, I lay by your side in a sandpit
and we pretended to be at the edge of the sea
where vowels were as smooth as hair.

5.

Holed up in the house, chair ensconced, sconces
land on three iron feet, fear stuffed down
in the corner, the bole of the tree seen
from the settee quivering in the dark—
myopically alive. Get out the flash, probe
the darkness, return to bed. Beds abet
loneliness unless someone else is also
from nighttime waking to hallucinated
mouth gaping and chewing its morts, orts,
legs and assorted limbs, moppets dripping
like truth to the floor. Goya's own moved in
from next door, where last seen, Kronos eating
his own children, my own mouthing stoned words,
a parody of speech and no sound, he
and his cronies grunt and hide, slither and shine,
wake unafraid, teenage puppies, six abed.

6.

If the chair doesn't move across polished floors
and tables aren't burning with electric pulse,
if I can't glide in patent shoes over turquoise tile,
why have you brought me here?
What reason for such straight lines,
such an ill-drawn moon?
When the cactus glows at night I'll swim the length
and hold my breath until the edge of the sea.
Once, in between one belief and another, I thought
this town's at the end of all waters.
Nobody lives here who isn't already taking notes.
Across from her at the counter a cowboy reads a script
and she responds with coy laughter.
Nothing happens. We take walks. Suddenly the slide.

The Contemporary Poetry Series

Edited by Paul Zimmer

Dannie Abse, *One-Legged on Ice*
Susan Astor, *Dame*
Gerald Barrax, *An Audience of One*
Tony Connor, *New and Selected Poems*
Franz Douskey, *Rowing Across the Dark*
Lynn Emanuel, *Hotel Fiesta*
John Engels, *Vivaldi in Early Fall*
John Engels, *Weather-Fear: New and Selected Poems, 1958-1982*
Brendan Galvin, *Atlantic Flyway*
Brendan Galvin, *Winter Oysters*
Michael Heffernan, *The Cry of Oliver Hardy*
Michael Heffernan, *To the Wreakers of Havoc*
Conrad Hilberry, *The Moon Seen as a Slice of Pineapple*
X. J. Kennedy, *Cross Ties*
Caroline Knox, *The House Party*
Gary Margolis, *The Day We Still Stand Here*
Michael Pettit, *American Light*
Bin Ramke, *White Monkeys*
J. W. Rivers, *Proud and on My Feet*
Laurie Sheck, *Amaranth*
Myra Sklarew, *The Science of Goodbyes*
Marcia Southwick, *The Night Won't Save Anyone*
Mary Swander, *Succession*
Bruce Weigl, *The Monkey Wars*
Paul Zarzyski, *The Make-Up of Ice*

The Contemporary Poetry Series

Edited by Bin Ramke

J. T. Barbarese, *New Science*
J. T. Barbarese, *Under the Blue Moon*
Scott Cairns, *The Translation of Babel*
Richard Cole, *The Glass Children*
Wayne Dodd, *Echoes of the Unspoken*
Wayne Dodd, *Sometimes Music Rises*
Joseph Duemer, *Customs*
Karen Fish, *The Cedar Canoe*
Caroline Knox, *To Newfoundland*
Patrick Lawler, *A Drowning Man Is Never Tall Enough*
Sydney Lea, *No Sign*
Phillis Levin, *Temples and Fields*
Gary Margolis, *Falling Awake*
Jacqueline Osherow, *Looking for Angels in New York*
Donald Revell, *The Gaza of Winter*
Martha Clare Ronk, *Desire in L.A.*
Aleda Shirley, *Chinese Architecture*
Susan Stewart, *The Hive*
Terese Svoboda, *All Aberration*
Arthur Vogelsang, *Twentieth Century Women*